JAN 2019

BREAKTHROUGHS IN
MARS
EXPLORATION

Lerner Publications Company
A division of Lerner Publishing Group, Inc.
241 First Avenue North
Minneapolis, MN 55401 USA

For reading levels and more information, look up this title at www.lernerbooks.com.

Main body text set in Aptifer Sans LT Pro Regular 12/18.
Typeface provided by Linotype AG.

Library of Congress Cataloging-in-Publication Data

Names: Kenney, Karen Latchana, author.
Title: Breakthroughs in Mars exploration / Karen Latchana Kenney.
Description: Minneapolis : Lerner Publications, [2019] | Series: Space exploration (Alternator books) | Audience: Ages 8-12. | Audience: Grades 4 to 6. | Includes bibliographical references and index.
Identifiers: LCCN 2018010734 (print) | LCCN 2018016777 (ebook) | ISBN 9781541543720 (eb pdf) | ISBN 9781541538696 (lb : alk. paper)
Subjects: LCSH: Mars probes—Juvenile literature. | Mars (Planet)—Exploration—Juvenile literature.
Classification: LCC TL799.M3 (ebook) | LCC TL799.M3 K46 2019 (print) | DDC 523.43—dc23
LC record available at https://lccn.loc.gov/2018010734

Manufactured in the United States of America
1-45052-35879-7/27/2018

Contents

SEVEN MINUTES OF TERROR

An artist's concept of NASA's *Mars Science Laboratory* spacecraft approaching Mars. The *Curiosity* rover is safely tucked inside the spacecraft.

The room was tense at NASA's mission control center. It was late at night on August 5, 2012, and millions of miles away in space, the *Curiosity* **rover** was landing on Mars.

The landing was risky. No one had attempted something like this before. First, a spacecraft holding the car-size rover hurtled through the **atmosphere** at 13,000 miles (20,920 km) per hour. A giant parachute opened above the spacecraft, and rockets fired to slow it down. Then the **heat shield** flew off, and the sky crane emerged.

The sky crane fired its rockets to hover above the surface of Mars. Then its cables slowly lowered the rover down onto the planet's red, rocky surface. "Touchdown confirmed. We're safe on Mars!" said a mission controller. It had been seven tense minutes for the technicians as they watched the landing. They erupted in cheers and high fives. After years of planning, *Curiosity* was finally on Mars.

Members of the team that worked on the *Curiosity* rover celebrate after the rover successfully landed on Mars.

THE MYSTERIOUS RED PLANET

This image of the north pole of Mars shows an icy region that is about 680 miles (1100 km) across.

Mars is one of the few planets we can see from Earth with just our eyes. People have always wondered about this red planet. They began looking at it with telescopes to see its landscape in more detail. They saw dark and light regions and white caps at its poles.

In 1877 Italian **astronomer** Giovanni Schiaparelli looked through his telescope and saw lines that seemed to crisscross the planet. Some people thought the lines were canals built by Martians. Other astronomers thought jungles might be on Mars. People began to wonder if Mars might be similar to Earth. Was there water and life there? People wanted to see Mars up close to find out more.

Giovanni Schiaparelli

NASA designed this probe, known as *Mariner 8*, to be the first to explore Mars. However, the probe broke down shortly after launch in 1971. *Mariner 9*, launched a few weeks later, successfully reached Mars.

A CLOSER LOOK

Beginning in the 1960s, NASA began sending spacecraft to get a better look at Mars. The first **probes** carried cameras and flew by the planet to take pictures. From these pictures, NASA scientists learned that Mars was a dry, rocky planet. It had canyons, craters, and ancient volcanoes, but no canals, liquid water, or visible life.

In 1975 NASA launched two *Viking* spacecraft. They would be the first to land on Martian soil. They carried instruments to test the soil and search for signs of life. The *Viking* landers didn't find life, but they did find evidence of water in the Martian soil. Photos from the *Viking* landers showed features that looked like ancient riverbeds. Other regions looked as if they had been formed by flooding.

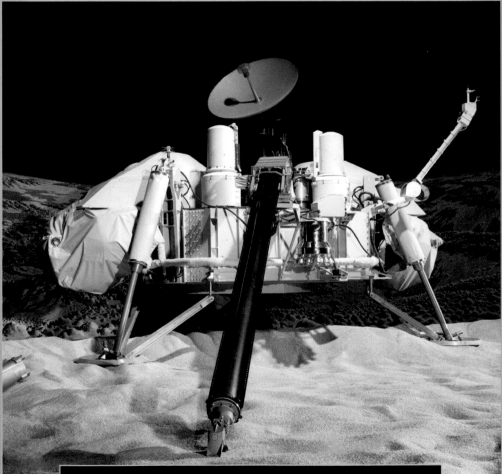

The first *Viking* spacecraft landed on Mars on July 20, 1976. It sent information to Earth for six years.

In 2001 the *Mars Odyssey* probe arrived at Mars. It **orbited** the planet for more than sixteen years. The probe completely mapped the planet and discovered evidence of ice below its surface.

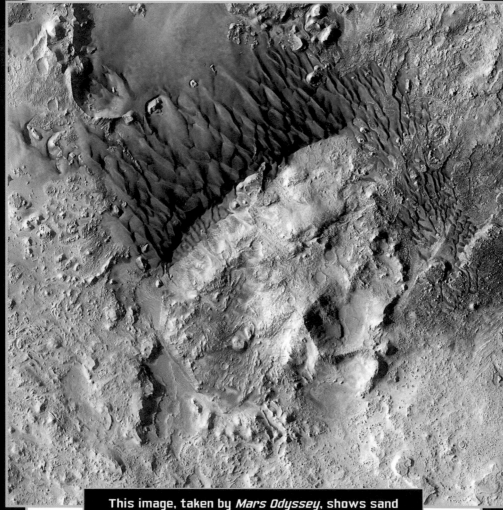

This image, taken by *Mars Odyssey*, shows sand dunes on the surface of Mars.

STEM FOCUS

A *Viking* photo showed a giant rock that had shadows shaped like two eyes, a nose, and a mouth. When NASA published the photo, people wondered if Martians had carved the rock long ago. In 1998 the *Mars Global Surveyor* probe used its high-tech camera to take another photo that was ten times clearer than the previous one. It revealed the rock to be only a mound with pits, bumps, and ridges.

Many people who saw this image of Mars thought the top feature looked like it had a face.

WATER, ICE, AND LIFE

The *Spirit* rover captured this image of itself on Mars two years after landing.

To study Martian soil and landscape further, NASA began sending rovers to the planet. *Spirit* and *Opportunity* landed on Mars in 2004. Scientists on Earth operated these remote-controlled robots. Their robotic arms had microscopes. Attached cameras allowed them to see the smallest parts of the rocks and soil they studied. These tools found clay and **minerals** that form only in water. The rovers were designed to last at least ninety days. But *Spirit*'s mission ended in 2011, and in February 2018, *Opportunity* reached five thousand Martian days working on the planet.

In the next decade, several more spacecraft arrived at Mars. The *Mars Express* probe studied the planet's polar caps. It found water ice and carbon dioxide ice at the planet's south pole. *Mars Express* also found small amounts of methane in the atmosphere. The gas is a common sign of life on Earth.

An artist's image shows *Mars Express* flying over Mars.

The *Mars Reconnaissance Orbiter* took this image of a canyon on Mars called Juventae Chasma.

The *Mars Reconnaissance Orbiter* searched for water too. Its advanced camera has taken some of the clearest images of Mars yet. Some images show what look like ancient steam vents. On Earth, underground water feeds these kinds of vents. Tiny living things live inside them on Earth. Scientists want to find out if the same is true on Mars.

CURIOUS FINDINGS

When *Curiosity* arrived on Mars in 2012, its mission was to find out whether Mars could support life. The rover was equipped with scientific instruments to scoop up soil and drill into rocks. *Curiosity* can also study these samples to find out what the rocks are made of and how they formed.

STEM FOCUS

The key ingredients for life include carbon, hydrogen, oxygen, phosphorus, and sulfur. *Curiosity* found all of these elements inside rocks on Mars. It also found methane in the atmosphere. *Curiosity* measured methane levels for two years. During two months, the levels of methane rose, so something on the planet produced it. Small living things, such as **bacteria**, could have made the methane. Or rocks might release methane when they react with water. Scientists don't know if the methane on Mars comes from living things or rocks.

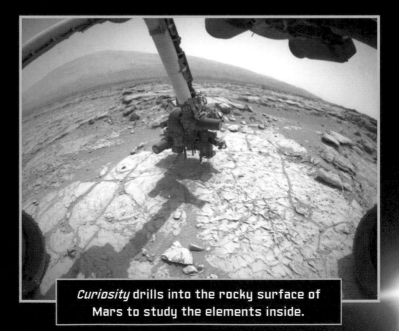

Curiosity drills into the rocky surface of Mars to study the elements inside.

Since 2014 the rover has been studying layers of rock and clay on a Martian mountain. NASA wants to learn how Mars has changed over time. In 2016 a motor on *Curiosity*'s drill stopped working, but NASA scientists figured out how to get the drill to work again. In 2018 *Curiosity* successfully drilled into a rock with the tool.

Curiosity also tracked weather patterns and **radiation** levels on Mars. Scientists wanted to determine whether a human mission to Mars would be possible. They believed that humans could not handle the radiation on Mars without special protection. They would use this information to plan future missions to Mars.

Curiosity climbs Vera Rubin Ridge on Mars. It is heading toward an area of clay that scientists are excited to study.

A MARS COLONY

NASA astronaut Scott Kelly has participated in studies to understand how space affects astronauts' bodies.

Scientists want to learn more than what rovers and spacecraft can tell us about Mars. NASA wants to send humans to live there. But many challenges need to be overcome before humans can even travel to Mars.

HUMAN RESEARCH

Being in space is hard on astronauts' bodies. Earth's **magnetic field** protects humans from harmful space radiation. But Mars does not have a magnetic field. Mars also has less **gravity**

Along with his yearlong mission on the International Space Station, Kelly participated in several other space missions. He has spent a total of 520 days in space.

than Earth. When astronauts go to space, their skeletons stretch, and their bones and muscles lose mass. A complete mission to Mars might take three years. So scientists want to know how the human body responds to long space missions.

In 2015 NASA sent astronaut Scott Kelly to live on the International Space Station. He stayed there for a year. His identical twin brother, Mark, stayed on Earth during the mission. Scientists ran tests on the twins before, during, and after the mission. During his year in space, Kelly experienced changes in his height, eyesight, and the bacteria in his digestive system. However, these changes quickly returned to normal when he was back on Earth.

Scientists also discovered longer-lasting changes to cells in Kelly's bones and immune system. Scientists will continue studying these changes to understand why they happened.

Scott Kelly (*left*) is reunited with his twin brother Mark Kelly on March 17, 2010.

NASA and other space agencies have also proposed building a space station near the moon called the Deep Space Gateway. After building the station, astronauts would travel there once per year. This would test humans' ability to live deep in space and help NASA plan longer space missions.

RESOURCES ON THE RED PLANET

Humans also need to prepare for other aspects of life in the Martian landscape. Very little oxygen is on Mars, no plants grow there, and water is not readily available. Bringing enough food, water, oxygen, and fuel to support a mission would be incredibly difficult.

Astronaut Peggy Whitson displays an experiment on the International Space Station that studies how plants grow in space.

Most spacecraft need thousands of gallons of fuel just to leave Earth's atmosphere. It would be very difficult for a spacecraft to carry enough fuel to get to Mars and back.

Fuel is heavy and takes up a lot of room in a spacecraft. Previous spacecraft traveling to Mars needed only enough fuel to get there. A human mission to Mars would also need enough fuel to get back home. Scientists are researching ways to make fuel from carbon dioxide and water. Fuel made on Mars could get astronauts back home.

NASA also wants to make it easier for future missions to survive on Mars. This means building landing pads, roads, and buildings on the planet. One NASA engineer is experimenting with robots that could 3D print concrete made of Mars dust.

Other researchers are looking at ways to produce food and water. Astronauts might be able to survive on the water found under the planet's surface. And they might be able to grow vegetables in greenhouses. Astronauts have already grown vegetables in space on the International Space Station. Scientists have also tested how plants react to Martian soil. First, they created a copy of Mars's soil. Then they used it to grow radishes, peas, tomatoes, and more. The vegetables grew well and were safe to eat.

These plants were part of an experiment testing how plants might grow on Mars.

Researchers in Hawaii lived in this dome for a year to study what life might be like in a Mars colony.

LIFE ON MARS

At first, just a few humans would go to Mars. They would need to work together to survive. Some researchers have begun testing what it might be like to live in a Mars colony. At the Hawaii Space Exploration Analog and Simulation habitat, a crew of researchers lived inside a 36-foot-wide (11 m) dome for months. They only left the dome in space suits for short visits outside to conduct experiments. These conditions model what astronauts' lives might be like on Mars. Scientists are studying how the researchers react to these living conditions. The results will help scientists understand the kinds of people that would work well together in a Mars colony.

2020 AND BEYOND

A technician works on part of the spacecraft that will carry the *Mars 2020* rover to Mars.

NASA plans to send another rover to Mars in 2020. *Mars 2020* will land just like *Curiosity*, with a sky crane lowering it to safety. This rover will search for past life and collect rock and soil samples. On a future mission, these samples could be brought back to Earth for further study in large laboratories.

The *Mars 2020* rover will also prepare for humans to set foot on Mars. The rover will test a method of making oxygen from Martian air for humans to breathe. And it will study the dust that blows across the planet to find out how it might affect structures and people living there.

An artist's image shows the *Mars 2020* rover on the surface of Mars, using its drill to collect samples of rocks and soil.

A SpaceX *Falcon Heavy* rocket lifts off from NASA's Kennedy Space Center in Florida on February 6, 2018.

MORE TO DISCOVER

NASA estimates it will be able to send humans to Mars in the 2030s. Some people think it will be sooner. SpaceX wants to get there by 2024. The company might do it. In February 2018, SpaceX successfully launched its powerful *Falcon Heavy* rocket. The spacecraft is designed to carry humans into space.

Mars is one of the most interesting and exciting space destinations. Humans have learned a lot about the planet through careful research. But there is much more to discover. The next few decades are sure to reveal more of the planet's secrets.

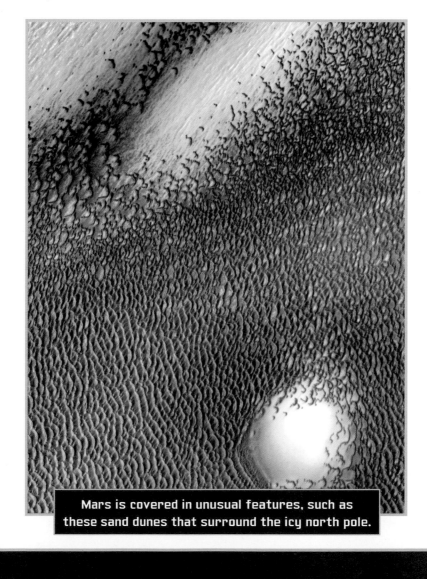

Mars is covered in unusual features, such as these sand dunes that surround the icy north pole.

Scientists continue to explore the red planet to
understand its mysteries. What will they discover next?

WHAT THE TECH?

The *Mars 2020* rover will be the most advanced rover yet. It will have new technology to help it land, move around, and analyze Mars. Its six wheels will be made of a new material that won't be damaged by rough terrain, and they will be better able to climb over tall rocks. A drill will collect rock and soil samples. And *Mars 2020* will be the first rover to have a microphone. So researchers will be able to hear sounds on the planet for the first time.

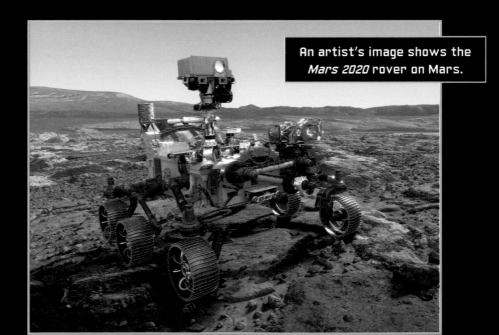

An artist's image shows the *Mars 2020* rover on Mars.

5 Mike Wall, "Touchdown! Huge NASA Rover lands on Mars." Space.com, August 6, 2012, https://www.space.com/16932-mars-rover-curiosity-landing-success.html.

GLOSSARY

astronomer: a scientist who studies the stars, planets, and space

atmosphere: the mix of gases that surround a planet

bacteria: tiny living things that live outside and inside creatures

gravity: the force that pulls things down to the surface of a planet

heat shield: an outer covering of a spacecraft that protects it from extreme heat

magnetic field: the area around a planet that is made by magnetism inside the planet, which protects it from harmful energy from the sun

minerals: substances that form naturally in the ground

orbited: traveled around something such as a planet in a curved path

probes: devices or machines used to explore or examine something

radiation: powerful energy that moves in invisible waves

rover: a vehicle that can drive on rough land and other planets

Aldrin, Buzz. *Welcome to Mars: Making a Home on the Red Planet.* Washington, D.C.: National Geographic, 2015.

Cornell, Kari. *Mars Science Lab Engineer Diana Trujillo.* Minneapolis: Lerner Publications, 2016.

Mars: The Red Planet
https://solarsystem.nasa.gov/planets/mars/overview/

Motum, Markus. Curiosity: *The Story of a Mars Rover.* Somerville, MA: Candlewick, 2018.

NASA: Mars for Kids
https://mars.nasa.gov/participate/funzone/

NASA: Mars 2020 Rover
https://mars.nasa.gov/mars2020/mission/rover/

National Geographic: Mars Rovers
https://video.nationalgeographic.com/video/mars-rovers-sci

Silverman, Buffy. *Mars Missions: A Space Discovery Guide.* Minneapolis: Lerner Publications, 2017.

INDEX

Photo Acknowledgments

Image credits: NASA/JPL-Caltech, pp. 4, 15; Brian van der Brug/Los Angeles Times/Getty Images, p. 5; NASA/JPL/MSSS, p. 6; Mondadori Portfolio/Getty Images, p. 7; NASA/JPL, pp. 8, 17, 18, 20, 24, 25, 26, 29; NASA/JPL-Caltech/University of Arizona, pp. 9, 14; NASA/JPL-Caltech/ASU, pp. 10, 27; CORBIS/Corbis/Getty Images, p. 11; NASA/JPL-Caltech/Cornell, p. 12; ESA/ATG medialab/DLR/FU Berlin (CC BY-SA 3.0 IGO), p. 13; NASA/JPL-Caltech/MSSS, p. 16; NASA/Rob Navias, p. 19; Science & Society Picture Library/Getty Images, p. 21; NASA/Dimitri Gerondidakis, p. 22; HI-SEAS V crew/University of Hawai'I, p. 23; NASA/JPL/USGS, p. 28; Design elements: filo/Getty Images; satit sewtiw/Shutterstock.com; Supphachai Salaeman/Shutterstock.com.

Cover: NASA/JPL-Caltech/MSSS.